Dessert Cookbook: F
Recipes for the Mediterranean Diet

by Vesela Tabakova
Text copyright(c)2014 Vesela Tabakova

Table of Contents

Delicious and Healthy Desserts for Any Occasion

It is hard to imagine a great family lunch without any dessert! Holidays, family gatherings, New Year's Eve, birthday parties and so on – these are events that remind us of the good cake, cookies or other brilliant desserts from our childhood. Sometimes, in this ever-complicated world of ours, we crave the simpler, nostalgic tastes of bygone times - the desserts of our childhood, made by loving hands, that never go out of style.

There is something special about traditional Mediterranean desserts - they are more elegant and healthy than most sweets and are simply amazing. What is even better is that preparing homemade Mediterranean desserts is easy enough for even the inexperienced cook!

Cherry Clafoutis

Serves 4

Ingredients:

1/2 cup flour

1/4 cup plus 2 tablespoons sugar

a pinch of salt

3 large eggs

3 tbsp unsalted butter, melted

zest of 1 lemon

1/4 cup plus 2 tbsp milk

3 cups cherries, pitted

1 tbsp Cognac or brandy (optional)

1 tsp vanilla extract

powdered sugar, for dusting

Directions:

Pit the cherries using a cherry pitter. Place then on a small tray in a single layer, sprinkle with 1/4 cup sugar and shake gently to coat. Place in the freezer for 1 hour or until firm.

Preheat the oven to 350 F. Butter a 9-inch gratin dish. In a bowl, whisk the flour, sugar, vanilla and a pinch of salt. Whisk in the eggs, melted butter, brandy and lemon zest. Beat until smooth. Add in the milk and continue whisking for about 3 minutes, until light and very smooth. Pour the batter into the dish and top with the cherries.

Bake for about 30 minutes, until the clafoutis is set and golden. Let cool slightly. Dust with powdered sugar.

Baklava - Walnut Pie

Serves 15

Ingredients:

14 oz filo pastry

1 cup ground walnuts

9 oz butter

For the syrup:

2 cups sugar

2 cups water

1 tbsp vanilla powder

2 tbsp lemon zest

Directions:

Grease a baking tray and place 2-3 sheets of filo pastry.
Crush the walnuts and spread some evenly on the pastry.
Place two more sheets of the filo pastry on top. Repeat until
all the pastry sheets and walnuts have been used up. Always
finish with some sheets of pastry on top.

Cut the pie in the tray into small squares. Melt the butter and pour it over the pie. Bake in a preheated oven at 390 F until light brown. When ready set aside to cool.

the syrup: Combine water and sugar in a saucepan. Add vanilla and lemon zest and bring to the boil, then lower the heat and simmer for about 5 minutes until the syrup is nearly thick. Pour hot syrup over the cold baked pie, set aside for at least 1-2 days until the syrup is completely absorbed.

Delicious French Eclairs

Serves 12

Ingredients:

1/2 cup butter

1 cup boiling water

1 cup sifted flour

4 eggs

a pinch of salt

Directions:

In a medium saucepan, combine butter, salt, and boiling water. Bring to the boil, then reduce heat and add a cup of flour all at once, stirring vigorously until mixture forms a ball.

Remove from heat and add eggs, one at a time, whisking well to incorporate completely after each addition. Continue beating until the mixture is thick and shiny and breaks from the spoon.

Pipe or spoon onto a lined baking sheet then bake for 20 minutes in a preheated to 450 F oven. Reduce heat to 350 F and bake for 20 minutes more, or until golden. Set aside to cool and fill with sweetened whipped cream or custard.

Chocolate Madeleines

Serves 12

Ingredients:

1/4 cup sifted flour

2 oz butter

1 egg

2 egg yolks

1/3 cup sugar

1/3 cup cocoa powder

1/2 tsp baking powder

a pinch of salt

1/2 tsp vanilla extract

1/2 cup powdered sugar, for dusting

Directions:

Sift the flour with cocoa, baking powder and salt in a large mixing bowl. In another bowl, beat the butter with the vanilla extract and the sugar. Mix in the egg and the egg yolks. Add in the dry ingredients, stirring, until just combined. Pour batter into buttered Madeleine shell forms.

Bake in a preheated to 375 F oven, for about 10 minutes. Remove from oven and immediately invert onto a wire rack to cool. Sprinkle with powdered sugar and serve.

Turkish Semolina Cake in Syrup

Serves 6-8

Ingredients:

3 eggs

½ cup sugar

1 cup yogurt

1 cup sunflower oil

3 tbsp flour

1 cup semolina

1 tsp vanilla powder

½ tsp baking soda

1 tbsp baking powder

½ tsp salt

1 tbsp grated lemon zest

for the syrup:

1 1/2 cups sugar

1 1/2 cups water

juice of half a lemon

Directions:

Put water and sugar in a pot and bring to a boil, stirring. Boil it for about 4-5 minutes, then add the lemon juice. Continue boiling for 2-3 minutes, then set aside to cool.

Beat very well eggs and sugar, yogurt and oil. Add the other ingredients, combining everything again.

Grease a square 8×8 inch pan and pour the batter in it. Bake it in a preheated to 350F oven for 25-30 min, until golden brown.

Pour the cold syrup over the warm dessert. Set aside to cool then place in the refrigerator for an hour. Serve cut in squares.

French Fruit Cake

Serves 12

Ingredients:

1/2 cup butter, softened

1/2 cup sugar

2 1/2 tbsp honey

2 eggs

3/4 cup candied orange peel

1/2 cup candied lemon peel

1/2 cup raisins

1/2 cup walnuts, chopped

1 1/2 cups flour

1/2 tsp baking powder

1 1/2 tbsp milk

2 tbsp dark rum

1 tsp vanilla extract

Directions:

In a large bowl, beat the butter with the sugar and honey. Add in the eggs, the milk, rum, and vanilla extract. Stir in the remaining flour and the baking powder.

Add the fruits and nuts and combine well. Turn the batter into a greased and floured 9 x 5 inch loaf pan.

Bake in a preheated to 350 F oven for 10 minutes. Lower the heat to 325 F and bake the cake for 40 minutes more, or until a toothpick comes out clean.

Easy Pear Tart

Serves 12

Ingredients:

1 cup butter, softened

1 cup sugar

4 eggs

2 cups flour

1 tsp baking powder

4 ripe pears, peeled and cubed

1 tsp vanilla extract

a pinch of salt

1 tsp lemon zest

Directions:

Grease a 9½ inch springform pan. Cream butter and sugar until very fluffy. Mix in the eggs slowly, one egg at a time. Add vanilla extract and lemon zest and stir. Add flour, baking powder and salt, stirring gently. Do not over mix.

Pour half of the batter into the pan then arrange the pears on top. Pour the rest of the batter over the pears. Bake in a preheated to 350 F oven for about 45 min or until a toothpick comes out clean.

Moist Apricot Muffins

Serves 16

Ingredients:

2 1/2 cups flour

1 cup white sugar

2 eggs

1 cup yogurt

1/2 cup milk

1/2 cup sunflower oil

2/3 cup apricots, chopped

1 tsp baking soda

1 tsp vanilla extract

1 tsp lemon zest

Directions:

Preheat oven to 400 F. Grease 16 muffin cups or line with paper muffin liners.

Combine flour, sugar, chopped apricots, vanilla and baking soda in a large bowl.

Whisk eggs, yogurt, milk, lemon zest and sunflower oil in another bowl until smooth; pour into dry mixture and stir until batter is just blended.

Fill prepared muffin cups 3/4 full and bake for 20 minutes or until a toothpick comes out clean. Cool in the pans for 10 minutes before removing to cool completely on a wire rack.

Bulgarian Cake

Serves 24

Ingredients:

3 eggs, beaten

1 cup sugar

1 cup yogurt

1/2 cup vegetable oil

1 tbsp baking powder

1 tbsp vanilla powder

1 tsp grated lemon rind

1 tbsp cocoa powder

3 cups flour

Directions:

Beat the eggs with the sugar and add the vegetable oil. Add in yogurt. Mix the baking powder with the flour and add it to the egg mixture along with vanilla and lemon rind.

Preheat the oven to 350 F and warm a 10 inch tube pan. Pour two thirds of the mixture into it. Add a tablespoon of cocoa powder to the remaining dough, mix well and pour it in the cake tin.

Bake for about 35 minutes or until a toothpick comes out clean.

Pumpkin Cake

Serves 12

Ingredients:

2 cups grated pumpkin

11/2 cup sugar

1 tsp cinnamon

1/2 cup sunflower oil

1 cup warm water

1 cup ground walnuts

3 cups flour

1 tbsp baking powder

Directions:

Mix sugar and grated pumpkin with cinnamon and leave for 15 minutes to absorb the aroma. Add oil and mix well with a fork. Add warm water and the crushed walnuts, stirring well.

Combine the baking powder with the flour and gently add to the dough.

Preheat oven to 350 F. Pour the dough in an oiled and floured 10 inch tube pan. Bake for about 35 minutes. When ready and cold turn over a plate and sprinkle with powdered sugar.

Apple Cake

Serves 12

Ingredients:

4-5 medium apples, sliced, cooked and mashed

1 cup walnuts, chopped

1/2 cup apple cider

1/2 cup sunflower oil

3 1/2 cups flour

1 1/2 cups sugar

1 tbsp baking powder

1/2 tsp baking soda

a pinch of salt

1 tsp cinnamon

1 /2 tsp fresh ground cardamom

1/2 tsp ground cloves

Directions:

Combine flour, baking powder, baking soda and salt. In another bowl, mix sugar, vegetable oil and apple cider, until well blended. Add in spices and stir again.

In a smaller bowl, mash cooked apples. Add apples to liquid ingredients and mix well. Add dry ingredients to wet ingredients, stirring. Add in walnuts and combine everything well.

Spread batter evenly in a lined 9×13 inch baking pan. Bake in a preheated to 350 F oven for 40 minutes. When completely cooled, dust with powdered sugar and cut.

Moroccan Lemon Cake

Serves 12

Ingredients:

4 eggs

1/2 cup milk

1 1/2 cups sugar

1/2 cup vegetable oil

2 cups flour

2 tbsp baking powder

a pinch of salt

2 tbsp fresh lemon juice

zest from 1 or 2 lemons

1 tsp vanilla powder

Directions:

Beat together eggs and sugar until creamy. Gently beat in the vegetable oil. Add in the flour, baking powder, a pinch of salt, and the milk. Whisk until smooth, then add in lemon juice, lemon zest and vanilla powder.

Pour the batter into a greased 10 inch tube pan and bake in a preheated to 350 F oven for about 40 minutes, or until a toothpick comes out clean. Set aside to cool then turn out onto a rack to finish cooling.

Almond Cake

Serves 10

Ingredients:

1-1/2 cups blanched whole almonds

6 large eggs, separated

1 cup powdered sugar

1 tbsp orange zest

1 tbsp lemon zest

3 drops almond extract

1/3 cup powdered sugar, for dusting

Directions:

Grind the almonds in a food processor very finely. Beat the egg yolks with the sugar until creamy. Beat in the lemon and orange zest together with the almond extract. Add in the ground almonds and beat until well combined.

In another bowl beat the egg whites until stiff peaks form. Fold them into the yolk mixture. Grease an 11-inch long loaf pan and dust it with flour. Pour in the cake batter, and bake in a preheated to 350 F oven for 30-40 minutes. Let cool before turning out then dust with powdered sugar.

Vegan Cake

Serves 12

Ingredients:

1/2 cup sugar

1 cup fruit jam

1 cup cool water

1/2 cup vegetable oil

1 tsp vanilla powder

½ tsp ground cinnamon

1 cup crushed walnuts

1 tsp baking soda

21/2 cups flour

Directions:

Mix the baking soda with the jam and leave for 10 min. Add sugar, water, oil, walnuts and flour in that order. Mix well and pour in a 10 inch tube pan.

Bake in a preheated to 350 F oven. When ready turn over a plate and sprinkle with powdered sugar.

Semolina Shortbread with Caramelised Peaches

Serves 10

Ingredients:

6 tbsp unsalted butter, softened, plus a bit extra to grease the pan

1/4 cup sugar

1 cup flour

5 1/4 cup fine semolina

1/2 tsp vanilla extract

7 oz mascarpone cheese

1 tbsp powdered sugar

for the caramelised peaches

2 tbsp unsalted butter

4 peaches, peeled, halved, stones removed, sliced

1 tbsp lemon juice

1 tbsp brandy

a pinch of salt

5 tbsp sugar

Directions:

Beat the butter and sugar together until creamy. Slowly add in the flour and semolina, vanilla and salt. Continue beating until all the ingredients are well combined.

Carefully pour the batter into a greased tart pan and bake in a preheated to 280 F oven for 30 minutes, or until cooked.

Melt butter in a large pan over medium heat. Add peaches, lemon juice, brandy and sugar and simmer, stirring, until golden and caramelized. Set aside to cool.

Beat the mascarpone with the sugar. Cut the cake into 6 pieces and spread mascarpone on each piece. Top with the caramelized peaches and drizzle with sauce from the pan.

Apple Pastry

Serves 8

Ingredients:

14 oz filo pastry

5-6 apples, peeled and cut

11/2 cup walnuts, coarsely chopped

2/3 cup sugar

6 tbsp vegetable oil

1 tbsp cinnamon

1/2 tsp vanilla powder

1/2 cup powdered sugar, for dusting

Directions:

Cut the apples in small pieces and mix with the walnuts, sugar, cinnamon and the vanilla. Place two sheets of pastry in the baking dish, sprinkle with oil and spread the filling on top.

Repeat this a few times finishing with a sheet of pastry. Bake for 20 minutes at medium heat. Let the Apple Pastry cool down and dust with the powdered sugar.

Pumpkin Pastry

Serves 8

Ingredients:

14 oz filo pastry

1 cups pumpkin, shredded

1 cup walnuts, coarsely chopped

1/2 cup sugar

6 tbsp sunflower oil

1 tbsp cinnamon

1 tsp vanilla powder

1/2 cup powdered sugar, for dusting

Directions:

Grate the pumpkin and steam it until tender. Cool and add the walnuts, sugar, cinnamon and the vanilla. Place a few sheets of pastry in the baking dish, sprinkle with oil and spread the filling on top.

Repeat this a few times finishing with a sheet of pastry. Bake for 20 minutes at 350 F. Let the Pumpkin Pie cool down and dust with the powdered sugar.

Strawberry Jam Crêpes

Serves 15

Ingredients:

3 eggs

1/4 cup sugar

2 cups plain flour

2 cups milk

1/2 orange, juiced

1/2 tsp vanilla

1/4 cup sunflower oil

1/2 cup strawberry jam

Directions:

Using an electric mixer, lightly beat eggs and sugar until well combined. Add 1/2 cup flour, 1 tablespoon at a time, beating well after each addition.

Slowly add remaining 1 1/2 cups flour and milk alternately until batter is smooth. Reduce mixer speed. Add orange juice, vanilla and a pinch of salt. Beat until batter is smooth.

Heat a 7 inch base crêpe pan or frying pan over medium heat. Brush pan with a little oil. Pour 2 1/2 tablespoon of batter into center of pan and swirl to coat base. Cook for 1 to 2 minutes or until base is golden. Turn and cook for 30 seconds. Transfer to a plate. Repeat with remaining batter, greasing pan between crêpes.

Spread 1 teaspoon jam over 1 crêpe. Roll crêpe up tightly. Repeat with remaining crêpes and jam. Layer crêpes on a serving plate. Serve sprinkled with powdered sugar.

Quick Peach Tarts

Serves 4

Ingredients:

1 sheet frozen ready-rolled puff pastry

1/4 cup light cream cheese spread

2 tablespoons sugar

a pinch of cinnamon

4 peaches, peeled, halved, stones removed, sliced

Directions:

Line a baking tray with baking paper. Cut the pastry into 4 squares and place them on the prepared tray. Using a spoon, mix cream cheese, sugar, vanilla and cinnamon. Spread over pastry squares. Arrange peach slices on top.

Bake in a preheated to 350 F oven for 10 minutes, or until golden.

Sweet Cheese Balls with Syrup

Serves 6

Ingredients:

3.5 oz feta or cottage cheese

3 eggs

1 cup flour

1 tsp baking soda

1 cup sunflower oil

for the syrup:

1 1/2 cups sugar

1 1/2 cups water

juice of half a lemon

Directions:

Put water and sugar in a pot and bring to a boil, stirring. Boil it for about 4-5 minutes, then add the lemon juice. Continue boiling for 2-3 minutes, then set aside to cool.

Mix the feta cheese with the eggs, then gradually add the flour and the baking soda. Shape dough into balls with a spoon and fry in hot sunflower oil until golden-brown. Arrange cheese balls in a plate and pour over them the already cooled syrup.

Semolina Dessert

Serves 5-6

Ingredients:

1 cup semolina

4 oz butter

2 tbsp pine nuts

for the syrup:

1 cup sugar

1 cup water

1 cup milk

Directions:

Mix semolina, butter and pine nuts in a large pot and cook them, stirring constantly, on medium-low heat until golden brown.

In another pot, mix the syrup ingredients and bring to the boil. Very slowly pour the syrup into the pot with the semolina, stirring with a spoon, for 4-5 minutes, or until the mixture leaves the sides of the pot.

Remove from the heat and set aside, covered, for 5 minutes. When cooled, put it on a plate upside down and serve in slices.

Bulgarian Rice Pudding

Serves 4-5

Ingredients:

1 cup short-grain white rice

6 tbsp sugar

1 1/2 cup water

1 1/2 cup whole milk

1 cinnamon stick

1 strip lemon zest

Directions:

Place the rice in a saucepan, cover with water and cook over low heat for about 15 minutes.

Add milk, sugar, a cinnamon stick and lemon zest and cook over very low heat, stirring frequently, until the mixture is creamy. Do not let it boil.

When ready, discard the cinnamon stick and lemon zest. Serve warm or at room temperature.

Coconut-flavored Rice Pudding with Figs

Serves 4

Ingredients:

1 1/2 cups short-grain white rice, rinsed

1/2 cup brown sugar

8 figs, halved

3 cups boiling water

1 1/2 cups shredded coconut

1 tsp salt

1 tbsp vanilla powder

Directions:

In a heavy saucepan, bring 1 ½ cup water to a boil, then add the rice, stirring, until it boils again. Reduce the heat and simmer for 7-8 minutes, until the water is absorbed and the rice is half-cooked.

In another bowl, pour 1/12 cups boiling water over the shredded coconut, sugar, and vanilla and let it soak for 20 minutes. Drain well and pour into the rice. Bring to a boil, reduce the heat and simmer until the rice is done. Stir in the figs and serve.

Pasta with Honey and Pistachios

Serves 2

Ingredients:

1 cup cooked small pasta, warm

1 tbsp pistachio nuts, finely ground

1 tbsp butter

2 tbsp honey

3 tbsp sugar

1/2 tsp orange zest

1/2 tsp rose water

Directions:

Combine well all the ingredients in a bowl and serve warm or room temperature.

Caramel Cream

Serves 8

Ingredients:

11/2 cup sugar

4 cups cold milk

8 eggs

2 tsp vanilla powder

Directions:

Melt 1/4 of the sugar in a non-stick pan over low heat. When the sugar has turned into caramel, pour it into 8 cup-sized ovenproof pots covering only the bottoms.

Whisk the eggs with the rest of the sugar and the vanilla, and slowly add the milk. Stir the mixture well and divide between the pots.

Place the 8 pots in a larger, deep baking dish. Pour 3-4 cups of water into the dish. Place the baking dish in a preheated to 280 F oven for about an hour and bake but do not let the water boil, as the boiling will overcook the cream and make holes in it: if necessary, add cold water to the baking dish.

Remove the baking dish from the oven; remove the pots from the dish. Place a shallow serving plate on top, then invert each pot so that the cream unmolds. The caramel will form a topping and sauce.

Dark Chocolate Mousse

Serves 4

Ingredients:

4 oz dark chocolate, broken into small pieces

2 tbsp butter

a pinch of salt

2 egg yolks

4 tbsp water

1 tbsp sugar

2/3 cup heavy cream, chilled

Directions:

Put chocolate together with butter, 2 tablespoons of water and a pinch of salt in a heatproof bowl. Set this bowl over a bigger saucepan full with simmering water. When the butter and chocolate start to melt, stir gently until smooth. Set aside to cool.

Beat egg yolks, sugar and 2 tablespoons of water in another heatproof bowl over the same saucepan of simmering water. Whisk it for about 3-4 minutes, until egg yolk mixture is hot to the touch. Pour the hot egg mixture into the warm chocolate mixture and gently stir until smooth. Set over a bowl of ice to chill, whisking constantly until mixture is slightly cooler then room temperature.

Beat the 2/3 cup heavy cream until it forms soft peaks. Place half of it into the chocolate mixture and gently fold it. Add in the remaining half and continue folding until nearly all the streaks have disappeared. Divide mousse into 4 glass serving bowls, refrigerate at least 2 hours and serve.

Yogurt-Strawberries Ice Pops

Serves 8-9

Ingredients:

3 cups yogurt

3 tbsp honey

2 cups strawberries, quartered

Strain the yogurt in a piece of cheesecloth or a clean white dishtowel. You can suspend it over a bowl or the sink. Combine the strained yogurt with honey.

Blend the strawberries with a blender then gently fold the strawberry puree into the yogurt mixture until just barely combined, with streaks remaining.

Divide evenly among the molds, insert the sticks and freeze for 3 to 4 hours until solid.

Blueberry Yogurt Dessert

Serves 6

Ingredients:

1/3 cup blueberry jam

1 cup fresh blueberries

2 tbsp powdered sugar

1 cup heavy cream

2 cups yogurt

1 tsp vanilla extract

Directions:

Strain the yogurt in a piece of cheesecloth or a clean white dishtowel. You can suspend it over a bowl or the sink.

In a large bowl, beat the cream and powdered sugar until soft peaks form. Add strained yogurt and vanilla and beat until medium peaks form and the mixture is creamy and thick.

Gently fold half the fresh blueberries and the blueberry jam into cream mixture until just barely combined, with streaks remaining. Divide dessert among 6 glass bowls, top with fresh blueberries and serve.

Fresh Strawberries in Mascarpone and Rose Water

Serves 4

Ingredients:

6 oz strawberries, washed

1 cup mascarpone cheese

1/2 teaspoon rose water

1/2 teaspoon vanilla extract

1/4 cup white sugar

Directions:

In a bowl, combine together the mascarpone cheese, sugar, rose water and vanilla.

Divide the strawberries into 4 dessert bowls. Add two dollops of mascarpone mixture on top and serve.

Dried Fruit Biscotti

Serves 30

Ingredients:

2 1/2 cups flour

11/2 cups sugar

3 eggs

2 egg yolks

1 tsp baking powder

1/2 tsp salt

1 tsp lemon zest

1 tbsp vanilla extract

1 1/2 cups dried fruit (cranberries, plums, apricots and raisins), chopped

1/2 cup nuts, chopped

powdered sugar, for dusting

Directions:

Preheat the oven to 350 F and line two baking sheets with parchment paper. In a medium bowl beat eggs, egg yolks and sugar until creamy. Add lemon zest and vanilla extract. Stir well. Add in baking powder and flour and mix until just blended. Stir in dry fruits and nuts.

Using floured hands, divide dough into 2 pieces. Shape each piece of dough into a long log. Place on the prepared baking sheets and bake for about 25 minutes, until dry and stiff, but not very darkened in colour.

Remove from the oven and let cool for about 15 minutes. Cut into 1/2 inch diagonal slices and place them on the baking tray. Bake at 320 F, for another 15-17 minutes, until golden brown and dry. Set aside to cool completely, dust with powdered sugar and store in airtight containers

Dark Chocolate Biscotti

Serves 30

Ingredients:

2 cups flour

1 cup brown sugar

4 tbsp cocoa powder

1/2 cup walnuts, coarsely chopped

4 oz dark chocolate, chopped

1 tsp baking powder

4 tbsp butter, softened

2 eggs

1 tbsp milk

1 tsp vanilla extract

a pinch of salt

Directions:

Preheat oven to 350 F and line baking sheets with parchment paper. Combine all dry ingredients without the nuts and chocolate. Add softened butter and mix it well with a wooden spoon or with hands.

In another bowl, whisk eggs and milk and add them to the dry mixture. Knead to form a smooth dough. Add walnuts and chocolate.

Using floured hands, divide dough into two pieces. Form each piece into a roll as long as your cookie sheet. Flatten slightly and bake for about 15 minutes, or until firm to the touch. Set aside to cool.

Cut the biscotti rolls diagonally into 1/2-inch thick slices. Arrange biscotti on the baking sheet and bake again for 6 to 10 minutes on each side. Slices should be lightly toasted. Let cool completely and store in an airtight container.

Granny's Honey Cookies

Serves 45-50

Ingredients:

3 cups flour

1 cup sunflower oil

2 eggs

1 cup sugar

1 cup honey

1/2 tsp cinnamon

1 1/2 tsp baking soda

1 tsp vanilla extract

1 egg white, to decorate

Directions:

Beat the eggs together with the sugar. In a medium bowl, stir the baking soda in a cup of honey. Add in the egg mixture, vanilla, cinnamon, and sunflower oil. Stir again. Gently add in flour. If the dough is too soft, wrap it in plastic and refrigerate for an hour.

Roll out dough until it is 1/4 inch thick. Cut into desired shapes and place on a greased baking tray, leaving 1 inch of space between cookies.

Bake in a preheated to 350 F oven for 7-8 minutes, or until slightly golden around the edges. While cookies are still hot, brush with beaten egg white and sprinkle with colored sugars or decorations of choice.

Let cool completely and store in an airtight container.

Hazelnut Cookies

Serves 24-30

Ingredients:

2 cups hazelnuts, toasted

1 cup sugar

4 egg whites

1/2 tsp salt

1 tsp vanilla extract

3 drops almond extract

Directions:

Preheat oven to 325 F. Line or grease a baking sheet. Blend nuts and sugar in a food processor until finely ground. Transfer into a large bowl.

In another bowl, beat egg whites and salt until stiff peaks form. Gently combine the egg whites and the nut mixture. Add vanilla, almond extract, and gently mix again.

Drop tablespoonfuls of the batter, 2 inches apart, on the prepared baking sheets. Bake the cookies for 20 minutes, or until golden brown. Set aside to cool, then transfer to a wire rack to cool completely.

Marzipan Cookies

Serves 25-30

Ingredients:

1 cup flour

1 cup rice flour

1 cup sugar

3/4 cup butter

2 egg yolks

½ tsp baking powder

milk, for kneading

for marzipan

1 cup almonds, finely ground

2 egg whites

2/3 cup sugar

1 tsp lemon juice

Directions:

Beat sugar and egg yolks in a medium bowl. In another bowl combine rice flour, flour and baking powder. Add in butter and mix everything with hands for 5 minutes.

Pour in egg mixture and knead to a hard dough using a little bit of milk. Refrigerate for 1 hour if time permits.

Prepare marzipan by mixing all the ingredients and kneading to a smooth dough.

Roll out the cookie dough until it is 1/4 inch thick. Spread a thin layer of marzipan over it. Cut out the cookies. Arrange them on a lined baking tray and bake in a preheated to 350 F oven for 15-20 minutes.

Date Pinwheels

Serves 40-50

Ingredients:

3 1/2 cups flour

1 cup butter, softened

1 1/2 cups sugar

1 cup brown sugar

3 eggs, whisked

1 tsp lemon zest

1/2 tsp salt

1 tsp vanilla extract

1 1/2 tsp baking soda

2 cups dates, pitted and chopped

½ cup water

1 cup walnuts, chopped

Directions:

Chop the dates and place them in a saucepan with the water and 1/2 cup sugar. Simmer gently over medium heat until the mixture is thick. Add lemon zest and chopped nuts. Mix well and let cool.

Cream together the butter, sugar and brown sugar until light and fluffy. Whisk eggs until thick and add them to the butter mixture, incorporating them well. Stir in 1 teaspoon of vanilla extract. In a separate bowl, sift the flour together with salt and baking soda. Add that to the butter mixture and stir until just combined.

Divide dough into 3 parts. Roll out 1 part at a time into a rectangle. Spread a thin layer of date filling. Roll up jelly roll fashion in waxed paper. Refrigerate for at least one hour.

Preheat the oven to 350 F. Slice the rolls into 1/4 inch thick cookies using a sharp knife and arrange them 2 inch apart on greased or lined with parchment paper baking sheets.

Bake for 10-12 minutes, or until golden around the edges. Let cool on baking sheets for 10 minutes, then remove to wire racks. When completely cooled, store in airtight containers.

Date and Walnut Cookies

Serves 30

Ingredients:

2 cups flour

1/4 cup sour cream

1/2 cup butter, softened

1 1/2 cups brown sugar

1/2 cup white sugar

1 egg

1 cup dates, pitted and chopped

1/3 cup water

1/4 cup walnuts, finely chopped

1/2 tsp salt

1/2 tsp baking soda

a pinch of cinnamon

Directions:

Cook the dates together with the white sugar and water over medium-high heat, stirring constantly, until mixture is thick like jam. Add in the nuts, stir and remove from heat. Leave to cool.

In a medium bowl, beat the butter and brown sugar. Stir in the egg and the sour cream. Sift the flour together with salt, baking soda and cinnamon and stir it into the butter mixture.

Drop a teaspoon of dough onto a cookie sheet, place 1/4 teaspoon of the filling on top of it and top with an additional 1/2 teaspoon of dough. Repeat with the rest of the dough. Bake cookies for about 10 minutes in a preheated to 340 F oven, or until golden.

Moroccan Stuffed Dates

Serves 30

Ingredients:

1 lb dates

1 cup blanched almonds

1/4 cup sugar

1 1/2 tbsp orange flower water

1 tbsp butter, melted

1/4 teaspoon cinnamon

Directions:

Process the almonds, sugar and cinnamon in a food processor. Add the butter and orange flower water and process until a smooth paste is formed.

Roll small pieces of almond paste the same length as a date. Take one date, make a vertical cut and discard the pit. Insert a piece of the almond paste and press the sides of the date firmly around.

Repeat with all the remaining dates and almond paste.

Fig Cookies

Serves 24

Ingredients:

1 cup flour

1 egg

1/2 cup sugar

1/2 cup figs, chopped

1/2 cup butter

1/4 cup water

1/2 tsp vanilla extract

1 tsp baking powder

a pinch of salt

Directions:

Cook figs with water, stirring, for 4-5 minutes, or until thickened. Set aside to cool. Beat butter with sugar until light and fluffy. Add in the egg and vanilla and beat to blend well.

In another bowl, sift together flour, baking powder and salt. Blend this into the egg mixture. Stir in the cooled figs.

Drop teaspoonfuls of dough on a greased baking tray. Bake in a preheated to 375 F oven, for about 10 minutes, or until lightly browned. Remove cookies and cool on wire racks.

Almond Cookies

Serves 25-30

Ingredient:

1 cup almonds, blanched, toasted and finely chopped

1 cup powdered sugar

4 egg whites

2 tbsp flour

1/2 tsp vanilla extract

1 pinch ground cinnamon

powdered sugar, to dust

Directions:

Preheat oven to 320 F. Blend the almonds in a food processor until finely chopped. Beat egg whites and sugar until thick. Add in vanilla extract and cinnamon. Gently stir in almonds and flour.

Place tablespoonfuls of mixture on two lined baking trays. Bake for 10 minutes, or until firm. Turn oven off, leave the door open and leave cookies to cool. Dust with powdered sugar.

Turkish Delight Cookies

Serves 48

Ingredients:

4 cups flour

3/4 cup sugar

1 cup lard (or butter)

3 eggs

1 tsp baking powder

1 tsp vanilla extract

8 oz Turkish delight, chopped

powdered sugar, for dusting

Directions:

Heat oven to 375 F. Line baking sheets with parchment paper. Beat the eggs well, adding sugar a bit at a time. Beat for at least 3 minutes, until light and fluffy. Melt the lard, then let it cool enough and slowly combine it with the egg mixture.

Mix the flour and the baking powder. Gently add the flour mixture to the egg and lard mixture to create a smooth dough. Divide dough into two or three smaller balls and roll it out until ¼ inch thick. Cut squares 3x2 inch.

Place a piece of Turkish delight in each square, roll each cookie into a stick and nip the end. Bake in a preheated to 350 F oven until light pink. Dust in powdered sugar and store in an airtight container when completely cool.

Anise Cookies

Serves 24

Ingredients:

1 ½ cups flour

1/3 cup sugar

1/3 cup olive oil

1 egg, whisked

3 tsp fennel seeds

1 tsp cinnamon

zest of one orange

3 tbsp anise liqueur

sugar, for sprinkling

Directions:

Heat olive oil in a small pan and sauté fennel seeds for 20-30 seconds. In a large bowl, combine together flour, sugar, and cinnamon. Add in olive oil, stirring, until well combined. Add orange zest and anise liqueur. Mix well then knead with hands until a smooth dough is formed. Add a little water if necessary.

On a well floured surface, form two 1 inch long logs. Cut 1/8 inch cookies, arrange them on greased baking sheets. Brush each cookie with egg and sprinkle with sugar. Bake cookies in a preheated to 350 F oven, for about 10 minutes, or until golden and crisp. Let cool, then store in an airtight container.

Spanish Nougat

Serves 20-24

Ingredients:

11/2 cup honey

3 egg whites

1 ¾ cup almonds, roasted and chopped

Directions:

Pour the honey into a saucepan and bring it to a boil over medium-high heat, then set aside to cool. Beat the egg whites to a thick glossy meringue and fold them into the honey.

Bring the mixture back to medium-high heat and let it simmer, constantly stirring, for 15 minutes. When the color and consistency change to dark caramel, remove from heat, add the almonds and mix trough.

Line a 9x13 inch pan with foil and pour the hot mixture on it. Cover with another piece of foil and even out. Let cool completely.

Place a wooden board weighted down with some heavy cans on it. Leave like this for 3-4 days, so it hardens and dries out. Slice into 1 inch squares.

Spanish Crumble Cakes

Serves 20-30

Ingredients:

2 cups flour

1 cup butter, softened

1 cup sugar

1 egg

1 tsp lemon zest

1 tsp orange zest

1 tbsp orange juice

1/2 cup almonds, blanched and finely ground

Directions:

Beat butter with sugar, lemon and orange zest until light. Stir in the flour, using a wooden spoon. Add ground almonds, stir, then knead with your hands until dough clings together. Divide it in three parts. Cover and refrigerate for at least half an hour.

On a well floured surface, roll out each piece of dough until it is 1/4 inch thick. Cut into different shapes. Arrange cookies on an ungreased baking sheet.

Beat together egg and orange juice and brush this over the cookies. Bake in a preheated to 350 F oven for 7-8 minutes, or until edges are lightly golden. Set aside to cool and store in an airtight container.

Greek Honey Cookies

Serves 40

Ingredients:

1 ¾ cups olive oil

2 cups walnuts, coarsely ground

1 cup sugar

1 cup fresh orange juice

3 tbsp orange peel

1/3 cup cognac

1 ½ tsp baking soda

1 tsp baking powder

sifted flour, enough to make soft oily dough

for the syrup

2 cups honey

1 cup water

for sprinkling

1 cup very finely ground walnuts

1 tsp ground cinnamon

1 tsp ground cloves

Directions:

Line 2 baking trays with baking paper. In a very large bowl, whisk together oil, sugar, orange zest, orange juice, cognac, baking soda, baking powder, and salt until well combined. Stir in flour with a wooden spoon until a soft dough is formed.

Roll tablespoonfuls of the mixture into balls. Place them, about 1.5 inch apart, on the prepared trays. Use a fork to decorate the top of each cookie by cross-pressing. Bake in a preheated to 350 F oven, for 30-35 minutes, or until golden.

Place the water and honey in a medium saucepan over medium-high heat. Simmer for 5 minutes, removing foam. Lower heat and with the help of a perforated spoon, dip 5-6 cookies at a time into the syrup.

Once the cookies have absorbed a little of the syrup, remove them with the same spoon and place them on a tray to cool and get rid of any excess syrup. When all the cookies have been dipped in the syrup, sprinkle with a mixture of cinnamon, cloves and finely ground walnuts.

Cinnamon Butter Cookies from Portugal

Serves 24

Ingredients:

2 cups flour

1/2 cup sugar

5 tbsp butter

3 eggs

1 tbsp cinnamon

Directions:

Cream the butter and sugar until light and fluffy. Combine the flour and the cinnamon. Beat eggs into the butter mixture. Gently add in the flour. Turn the dough onto a lightly floured surface and knead just once or twice until smooth.

Form a roll and divide it into 24 pieces. Line baking sheets with parchment paper or grease them. Roll each piece of cookie dough into a long thin strip, then make a circle, flatten a little and set it on the prepared baking sheet.

Bake cookies, in batches, in a preheated to 350 F oven, for 12 to 15 minutes. Set aside to cool on a cooling rack.

Best French Meringues

Serves 36

Ingredients:

4 egg whites

2 1/4 cups powdered sugar

Directions :

Preheat the oven to 200 F. and line a baking sheet.

In a glass bowl, beat egg whites with an electric mixer. Add in sugar a little at a time, while continuing to beat at medium speed. When the egg white mixture becomes stiff and shiny like satin, transfer to a large pastry bag.

Pipe the meringue onto the lined baking sheet with the use of a large round tip or star tip.

Place the meringues in the oven and and leave the oven door slightly ajar. Bake for 2 1/2 hours, or until the meringues are dry, and can easily be removed from the pan.

Cinnamon Palmiers

Serves 30

Ingredients:

1/3 cup granulated sugar

2 tsp cinnamon

1/2 lb puff pastry

1 egg, beaten (optional)

Directions:

Stir together the sugar and cinnamon. Roll the pastry dough into a large rectangle. Spread the cinnamon sugar in an even layer over the dough.

Starting at the long ends of the rectangle, loosely roll each side inward until they meet in the middle. If needed, brush it with the egg to hold it together. Slice the pastry roll crosswise into 1/4-inch pieces and arrange them on a lined with parchment paper baking sheet.

Bake cookies in a preheated to 400 F oven for 12-15 minutes, until they puff and turn golden brown. Serve warm or at room temperature.

Honey Sesame Cookies

Serves 25-30

Ingredients:

3 cups flour

1 cup sugar

1 cup butter

2 eggs

3 tbsp honey

1 cup pistachio nuts, roughly chopped

1 cup sesame seeds

1 tbsp vinegar

1 tsp vanilla

1 tsp baking powder

a pinch of salt

Directions:

Cream the butter and the sugar until light and fluffy. Gently add in the eggs, then the vanilla extract and the vinegar. Combine the flour, salt, and baking powder and add it to the butter mixture. Beat until just incorporated. Cover and refrigerate for an hour.

Mix the sesame seeds and the honey in a medium plate. Place the pistachios in another one. Take a teaspoonful of dough, form it into a ball, then dip it into the pistachios. Flatten it a little and dip it into the sesame-honey mixture. Repeat with the remaining dough, arranging the cookies on a lined baking sheet.

Bake the cookies in a preheated to 350 F oven for 15 minutes, or until they turn light brown. Set aside to cool on the baking sheet for 2-3 minutes then move to a wire rack.

Baked Apples

Serves 4

Ingredients:

8 medium sized apples

1/3 cup walnuts, crushed

3/4 cup sugar

3 tbsp raisins, soaked in brandy or dark rum

vanilla, cinnamon according to taste

2 oz butter

Directions:

Peel and carefully hollow the apples. Prepare stuffing by beating the butter, 3/4 cup of sugar, crushed walnuts, raisins and cinnamon.

Stuff the apples with this mixture and place them in an oiled dish. Sprinkle the apples with 1-2 tablespoons of water and bake in a moderate oven.

Serve warm with a scoop of vanilla ice cream.

Pumpkin Baked with Dry Fruit

Serves 5-6

Ingredients:

1.5 lb pumpkin, cut into medium pieces

1 cup dry fruit (apricots, plums, apples, raisins)

1/2 cup brown sugar

Directions:

Soak the dry fruit in some water, drain and discard the water. Cut the pumpkin in medium cubes.

At the bottom of a pot arrange a layer of pumpkin pieces, then a layer of dry fruit and then again some pumpkin. Add a little water.

Cover the pot and bring to boil. Simmer until there is no more water left. When almost ready add the sugar. Serve warm or cold.

FREE BONUS RECIPES: 10 Ridiculously Easy Jam and Jelly Recipes Anyone Can Make

A Different Strawberry Jam

Makes 6-7 11 oz jars

Ingredients:

4 lb fresh small strawberries (stemmed and cleaned)

5 cups sugar

1 cup water

2 tbsp lemon juice or 1 tsp citric acid

Directions:

Mix water and sugar and bring to the boil. Simmer sugar syrup for 5-6 minutes then slowly drop in the cleaned strawberries. Stir and bring to the boil again. Lower heat and simmer, stirring and skimming any foam off the top once or twice.

Drop a small amount of the jam on a plate and wait a minute to see if it has thickened. If it has gelled enough, turn off the heat. If not, keep boiling and test every 5 minutes until ready. Two or three minutes before you remove the jam from the heat, add lemon juice or citric acid and stir well.

Ladle the hot jam in the jars until 1/8-inch from the top. Place the lid on top and flip the jar upside down. Continue until all of the jars are filled and upside down. Allow the jam to cool completely before turning right-side up. Press on the lid to check and see if it has sealed. If one of the jars lids doesn't pop up- the jar is not sealed–store it in a refrigerator.

Raspberry Jam

Makes 4-5 11 oz jars

Ingredients:

4 cups raspberries

4 cups sugar

1 tsp vanilla extract

1/2 tsp citric acid

Directions:

Gently wash and drain the raspberries. Lightly crush them with a potato masher, food mill or a food processor. Do not puree, it is better to have bits of fruit. Sieve half of the raspberry pulp to remove some of the seeds. Combine sugar and raspberries in a wide, thick-bottomed pot and bring mixture to a full rolling boil, stirring constantly. Skim any scum or foam that rises to the surface. Boil until the jam sets.

Test by putting a small drop on a cold plate – if the jam is set, it will wrinkle when given a small poke with your finger. Add citric acid, vanilla, and stir. Simmer for 2-3 minutes more, then ladle into hot jars. Flip upside down or process 10 minutes in boiling water.

Raspberry-Peach Jam

Makes 4-5 11 oz jars

Ingredients:

2 lb peaches

1 1/2 cup raspberries

4 cups sugar

1 tsp citric acid

Directions:

Wash and slice the peaches. Clean the raspberries and combine them with the peaches is a wide, heavy-bottomed saucepan. Cover with sugar and set aside for a few hours or overnight. Bring the fruit and sugar to a boil over medium heat, stirring occasionally. Remove any foam that rises to the surface.

Boil until the jam sets. Add citric acid and stir. Simmer for 2-3 minutes more, then ladle into hot jars. Flip upside down or process 10 minutes in boiling water.

Blueberry Jam

Makes 4-5 11 oz jars

Ingredients:

4 cups granulated sugar

3 cups blueberries (frozen and thawed or fresh)

3/4 cup honey

2 tbsp lemon juice

1 tsp lemon zest

Directions:

Gently wash and drain the blueberries. Lightly crush them with a potato masher, food mill or a food processor. Add the honey, lemon juice, and lemon zest, then bring to a boil over medium-high heat. Boils for 10-15 minutes, stirring from time to time. Boil until the jam sets.

Test by putting a small drop on a cold plate – if the jam is set, it will wrinkle when given a small poke with your finger. Skim off any foam, then ladle the jam into jars. Seal, flip upside down or process for 10 minutes in boiling water.

Triple Berry Jam

Makes 4-5 11 oz jars

Ingredients:

1 cup strawberries

1 cup raspberries

2 cups blueberries

4 cups sugar

1 tsp citric acid

Directions:

Mix berries and add sugar. Set aside for a few hours or overnight. Bring the fruit and sugar to the boil over medium heat, stirring frequently. Remove any foam that rises to the surface. Boil until the jam sets. Add citric acid, salt and stir.

Simmer for 2-3 minutes more, then ladle into hot jars. Flip upside down or process 10 minutes in boiling water.

Red Currant Jelly

Makes 6-7 11 oz jars

Ingredients:

2 lb fresh red currants

1/2 cup water

3 cups sugar

1 tsp citric acid

Directions:

Place the currants into a large pot, and crush with a potato masher or berry crusher. Add in water, and bring to a boil. Simmer for 10 minutes. Strain the fruit through a jelly or cheese cloth and measure out 4 cups of the juice. Pour the juice into a large saucepan, and stir in the sugar. Bring to full rolling boil, then simmer for 20-30 minutes, removing any foam that may rise to the surface. When the jelly sets, ladle in hot jars, flip upside down or process in boiling water for 10 minutes.

White Cherry Jam

Makes 3-4 11 oz jars

Ingredients:

2 lb cherries

3 cups sugar

2 cups water

1 tsp citric acid

Directions:

Wash and stone cherries. Combine water and sugar and bring to the boil. Boil for 5-6 minutes then remove from heat and add cherries. Bring to a rolling boil and cook until set. Add citric acid, stir and boil 1-2 minutes more.

Ladle in hot jars, flip upside down or process in boiling water for 10 minutes.

Cherry Jam

Makes 3-4 11 oz jars

Ingredients:

2 lb fresh cherries, pitted, halved

4 cups sugar

1/2 cup lemon juice

Directions:

Place the cherries in a large saucepan. Add sugar and set aside for an hour. Add the lemon juice and place over low heat. Cook, stirring occasionally, for 10 minutes or until sugar dissolves. Increase heat to high and bring to a rolling boil.

Cook for 5-6 minutes or until jam is set. Remove from heat and ladle hot jam into jars, seal and flip upside down.

Oven Baked Ripe Figs Jam

Makes 3-4 11 oz jars

Ingredients:

2 lb ripe figs

2 cups sugar

1 ½ cups water

2 tbsp lemon juice

Directions:

Arrange the figs in a Dutch oven, if they are very big, cut them in halves. Add sugar and water and stir well. Bake at 350 F for about one and a half hours. Do not stir. You can check the readiness by dropping a drop of the syrup in a cup of cold water – if it falls to the bottom without dissolving, the jam is ready. If the drop dissolves before falling, you can bake it a little longer. Take out of the oven, add lemon juice and ladle in the warm jars. Place the lids on top and flip the jars upside down. Allow the jam to cool completely before turning right-side up.

If you want to process the jams - place them into a large pot, cover the jars with water by at least 2 inches and bring to a boil. Boil for 10 minutes, remove the jars and sit to cool.

Quince Jam

Makes 5-6 11 oz jars

Ingredients:

4 lb quinces

5 cups sugar

2 cups water

1 tsp lemon zest

3 tbsp lemon juice

Directions:

Combine water and sugar in a deep, thick-bottomed saucepan and bring it to the boil. Simmer, stirring until the sugar has completely dissolved. Rinse the quinces, cut in half, and discard the cores. Grate the quinces, using a cheese grater or a blender to make it faster. Quince flesh tends to darken very quickly, so it is good to do this as fast as possible. Add the grated quinces to the sugar syrup and cook uncovered, stirring occasionally until the jam turns pink and thickens to desired consistency, about 40 minutes. Drop a small amount of the jam on a plate and wait a minute to see if it has thickened. If it has gelled enough, turn off the heat. If not, keep boiling and test every 2-3 minutes until ready.

Two or three minutes before you remove the jam from the heat, add lemon juice and lemon zest and stir well.

Ladle in hot, sterilized jars and flip upside down.

About the Author

Vesela lives in Bulgaria with her family of six (including the Jack Russell Terrier). Her passion is going green in everyday life and she loves to prepare homemade cosmetic and beauty products for all her family and friends.

Vesela has been publishing her cookbooks for over a year now. If you want to see other healthy family recipes that she has published, together with some natural beauty books, you can check out her Author Page on Amazon.

Printed in Great Britain
by Amazon